ज़िन्दगी के Pages Hinglish मे....

Touching chapters of life through Hindi and English Poems

Prarthana Mukherjee

BookLeaf Publishing
India | USA | UK

Made with ❤ on the BookLeaf Publishing Platform
www.bookleafpub.in
www.bookleafpub.com

Dedication

I would like to dedicate this book to my family. My parents, my sister , my grand parents, my daughter and my husband.

Preface

Life is unique but certain emotions, a few experiences that we all go through during the journey of growing up is quite similar. This book tries to touch all the phases of nervousness, joy, ecstasy using a combination of both Hindi and English Poems.

We all have read Hindi and English Poems as a child, this book slowly navigates through our inner emotions with first touching the interpretation of God / भगवान and then sailing through life. All major life events starting from birth to the different first time experiences have been ornamented like a song.

These poems are sure to make you feel nostalgic,feel positive and bring a smile on your face.

Enjoy Reading!!!

Acknowledgements

My mother has been my inspiration. My family has been my strength. I acknowledge their immense contribution in inspiring me to write.

My workplace, my friends, good and not so great experiences also gave me ideas to write this book.

My emotional transactions during each phase have contributed in devising each poem.

Last but not the least, I am grateful to Bookleaf publication to come up with the idea of writing poems and publishing it giving a beautiful medium all the hidden poets and writers.

1. भगवान का अर्थ

भूमि है जिसका मूल आधार,
जिनसे उत्पन्न है अन्न और आहार।

गगन के सामान है जिसकी काया ,
जो है हर जीव की छाया।

वायु से करे जो हर प्राण का संचार,
हर गति का है वो आधार।

अग्नि के ताप से करते जीवन का जन्म और अंत,
तप और ताप का है वो स्तोत्र अनंत।

नीर से सींचा है जिसने हर जीव के प्राण,
उन्ही पंच महाभूतों के स्वामी कहलाते हैं "भगवान"।

2. Her Life

When she opened her eyes,
Hugged in warmth and light.
Step by step her senses combined,
To see, feel, touch and experience all that she could find.

Puzzled by events she started to grow,
Sometimes happy, sometimes with tantrums to throw,
Life had its own journey to show,
Some easy, some hard lessons to know.

Her heart was soft, mind strong,
Brain sharp as a knife to take over every storm.
She grew up to a young lady,
A loving friend,tough foe and a kind fairy.

She did good for whoever she could,
Got betrayed, fooled, at times rewarded as she should,
But life isn't easy, she understood.

She told herself and her inner voice,

How you lead your life is your choice.
Life is a journey you go alone,
Feel the roses and also cherish the stones.

For those who learn to be happy on their own,
Are invincible and are emperors without a throne!!!

3. असर जिंदगी का

ज़िन्दगी के सफर में ,
मोड़ है कितने सारे,
बदलते मौसम जैसे,
बदले तक़दीर हमारे ।

कांटो के दामन पर ही ,
खिलती खुशियों की हर कली ,
जब तलक समझे इंसान ,
हो जाती है ज़िन्दगी की शाम ।

पर मेरे दोस्त ये याद रख ,
असर ज़िन्दगी का है तब तक,
जब तक ये दिल देती है सीने पर दस्तक ।

4. Thoughts of a child

Hello , who am I,
Where am I,
Who is this lady ,
She feels like a fairy.

Her heartbeat makes me calm,
I feel secured when I am in her arms.
Now I have started to roll and crawl,
Why everyone is behind me after all?

I understand a little what they talk,
I mumble, stumble,giggle and try to walk.

Now that I am on my feet,I want to run,
Exploring the world has just begun.

Why eating is so important for a mother,
I want to play! just don't bother.

Grown ups are so lucky,they can go anywhere !

Do what they like and don't need any care.

When will parents understand,
Fun, Play,toys are what we have in our land!

5. जीवन क्या है

क्या है ये साँसों कि माला ,
या है कोई सपना प्यारा ,
बातों का है सिलसिला ,
या फिर ख़ामोशी का ज़लज़ला ।

नज़रों के सामने रंगो कि बौछार ,
या रंग खुद करता है आँखों का श्रृंगार
आवाज़ों कि गूंज से भर रहा है मन ,
धुनों कि बारिश में भीग रहा है तन ।

जीवन क्या है क्या जान सका है कोई यहां ?
बस देखा, सुना महसूस किया है ये अनोखा कारवां ।

6. Birth of a Mother

With a new life, a child, a mother is born,
Filled with bliss and fears, she cherishes this bond.

She feels the life within, each day,
Two bodies in one, takes this foray.
As time starts to flow,
She feels the Kicks and starts to glow.
Sleepless nights, difficult walk on days,
Life gets tougher, still she silently prays.

On the day the baby arrives,
Prayers answered, the new life thrives.

Now a new journey has begun,
No less struggle,many battles to be won.

Tiny fingers, loud cries,
Two souls renewing their ties.

What the world doesn't know,

Mother is equally frightened but unable to show.
With a child a mother is also born,
After all, the two souls were in one.
With fears,confusion yet wants to give the best she can,
Tears of joy, doubts in mind, her journey began.

Baby becomes a toddler, child , then a young lady or a man,
Mother's life becomes a boundless adventure land.
She is the nurturer, the teacher and the shield,
She knows and she has to bring in the warrior for the battlefield.

Once a mother, always a mother as they say
Mother's life is a unique foray,

When a MOTHER is born,
Her as life becomes a storm.

Let us understand that she is facing alone,
As she also needs understanding from whoever she calls her own.

7. Leaving Home...

Leaving home for the first time,
Thousands of thoughts crosses your mind.

Dreamy eyes, uncertain about the future,
How life is about to unfold in this new juncture.

Leaving the loving shadow of parents and being on your own,
Life beholds new experiences while learning to be alone.

What will I do,what will I need?
To sail through and to succeed!!

As you ask yourself and wreck your nerves,
Having faith in yourself brings you what you deserve.

Leaving home teaches you the actual chapter of life,
How to wander , find your way and to thrive!!!

8. स्कूल का पहला दिन

पता नहीं कहाँ ले जा रही है माँ ,
मेरे खिलौनों को छोड़कर, ये कौन सा है नया कारवां ।

अच्छी भली थी घर में मै तुम्हारे साथ ,
क्यों करूँ मै अनजान जगह पर अजनबियों से बात ।

तुमसे बिछड़कर स्कूल में क्यों जाऊं ,
तुम्हारे लाड की ख़ुशी वहाँ मै कैसे पाऊं ।

रोकूं कैसे अपने आंसू जब आएगी तुम्हारी याद,
जल्दी आ जाना लेने , कुछ देर बाद ।

ये कितने सारे बच्चे है मेरे जैसे,
कोई रोता हुआ, तो किसी के आंसुओं से भरे चेहरे ।
इनको भी आ रही है अपने घर की याद,
क्यों न मै इन्ही से कर लूं थोड़ी देर बात ।

इतने में माँ के जैसी एक टीचर आयीं,
"क्यों रोते हो सब ", कहकर धीमे से मुस्कराई ।
खेलेंगे हम साथ मिलकर , सीखेंगे नयी बातें ,

आओ मिलकर खेले ,कुछ सीखें ,खुशी भरे पल काटें ।

ये सुनकर सब बच्चों के जान में आयी नई जान ,
चलो सब मिलकर करे एक दूसरे से पहचान ।

लग रहा था जो स्कूल काँटों से भरा ,
धीमे धीमे बन गया वो खुशियों का नया बसेरा ।

9. दोस्ती का एहसास

दोस्ती का एहसास है कितना अनोखा ,
कुछ लोग ऐसे जो करते हैं जीवन को पूरा ।
बचपन के खेल हो या फिर ज़िन्दगी के मुश्किल मोड़ ,
दोस्तों के साथ से मिलता है हर मुश्किल का तोड़ ।

जो ढूंढ ले हंसी में गम के साज़ ,
और आंसुओं में छुपे राज़ ,
दोस्ती के जादू का है कुछ अलग ही अंदाज़ ।

चाहे रोज़ मिले या सालों बाद हो अचानक मुलाक़ात ,
वही ख़ुशी, वही जूनून मिलने पर होते हैं वही जज़्बात ।

जो कहा न जाए किसी से भी ,
वो कहते है दोस्ती में बेझिझक ,मस्ती में ,
खुशनसीब है वो जिन्हे मिलते है ऐसे दोस्त ज़िन्दगी में ।

10. Stepping into Office

Again a new world,again a new life,
"Office" is the new stepping stone, a new color of light!!

Feels like the first day of School,
Where you are nervous but still keep your cool!

You can see eyes scanning you while they show you the way,
Many ears trying to hear whatever you say.

Then you are shown a new desk and a cubicle,
Time to start a new foray, a new chronicle.
Thousands of thoughts blow your mind,
What to say, what to do and how to unwind.

Its that time of the life again,
Where you need to prove yourself and cross the terrain.

There would be many who would create roadblocks,
A calm and sharp mind only will cut through these

rocks.

Questions, expectations, all unfold,
As you take on this new role!!

Remember dear, nothing comes for free,
Success comes to those who stand as tall as tree,

Its also important to sway when winds are strong,
Gulp away the fear and ego ,
And gently pass through the storm.

Office life has its own challenges, might and power,
Brings hardships but also has many blessings to shower.

11. ससुराल का पहला दिन

गेंदे का फूल हो या काँटो वाले गुलाब ,
क्या है ये ससुराल या नया सैलाब ,
माता पिता कि वो नन्ही परी ,
आ गई है अब एक अनजान नगरी ,
आँखों में उम्मीद, मन में डर ,
दिमाग में एक ही सवाल ?
कैसा होगा मेरा ससुराल !

पहले दिन जब अक्षत छलकाए बढ़ाए अपने पाँव ,
सोचा मैंने क्या मिलेगी कड़कती धूप या ठंडी छाँव ।
शक़ के गरजेंगे बादल, या मिलेगा विश्वास का आँचल ।

क्या मिलेगा सम्मान और प्यार ,
या होगी कोई अलग झंकार ।

पहला दिन हर बड़े पड़ाव का होता है मुश्किल ,
कितने नज़र होते हैं आप पर,घबराया रहता है दिल ।
रिश्ते नातो का है एक नया सवेरा ,
अजनबियों से बन रहा है नया बसेरा ।

ऐसे में ,माँ की बातें आ रही थी याद,
"कभी न छोड़ना तुम अच्छाई का साथ !
बाँटो खुशियां सब में , रखो अपने मन में प्यार और सम्मान ,
अपनी कोशिशों से बना पाओगी नए घर में भी प्यार भरा मकाम !"

12. Happy being Alone

The joy of loneliness ,
When you find"YOU" is happiness!!

We meet so many souls on the way,
Each has a lesson and role to play,
Some teach you love,
Some make you strong!
And some , just walk along!!
Some bring joy and laughter,
Some invoke pain and anger.

But each one has a role to play,
To make you rock or soft as clay.

When time runs out in the cloud of life,
In the struggle to get success & to thrive!
You take a pause and think,
life moved fast as we blinked.

That's the time you understand,

Being alone is precious to find.
And as you grow old, you also realize,
You are the only one by your side.

13. Job Life!

Sustaining a job comes with its own struggle,
What to do right and how to juggle?

Clock has no value after you enter,
You have a time to get in but no fixed time to surrender!
Does working hard really bring success?
"Yes" only if you are in a team that is "HONEST"

If you fall into the tribe of wolves,
becomes hard to sustain the sharp hooks.

As you never know when you will be trapped,
And brushed slowly under the mat!

Office stress is not because of work,
Dealing politics and sailing through muck.

Proving yourself with unwanted blocks,
Needs a heart and mind made of rock.

You also meet some angels amidst the pessimistic crowd,
Who make you feel valuable and proud.

Life is not a bed of roses, it also has thorns they say,
Job life teaches you literally during it's foray!

14. बेपरवाह बचपन

कितने बेपर्वा थे बचपन के वो दिन,
हमेशा झूमता खिला रहता था मन !

आँखों में हज़ारों सपने ,
खुशियों के रंग भर देते थे अपने ।
न कोई चिन्ता न कल का डर ,
कब क्या होगा , इसकी न कभी होती थी फिकर ।

जीवन लगता था सर्कस का खेल,
हर पल चलती थी मौज की रेल ।
कभी बारिश में भीगना ,
कभी खेलते हुए गिरना ,
पड़ोसी के घर का खाना ,
लगता था मज़ेदार और अपना ।

बगीचे में उड़ती तितलियों के रंग,
भर देते थे दिल में नयी उमंग ।
इकट्ठे बैठकर देखते थे टीवी ,
कभी चित्रहार तो कभी वीसीआर पर मूवी ।

देखते देखते बीत गए वो बेपरवाह बचपन की आहटें ,
पर यादें अभी भी देती हैं सुकून और मुस्कराहटें ।

15. माँ बेटी

बेटी होती है सर का ताज ,
प्यारी लगती उसकी हर एक बात ।
छोटे से कदम जब चलने लग जाते हैं ,
मानो खुद की धड़कन बाहर घूमने लग जाते है ।

जब बीमार पड़े वो ,तो निकले खुद की जान ,
हर एक पल बन जाता मुश्किलों का तूफ़ान ।
जब धीरे धीरे लौट आये उसकी चेहरे की मुस्कराहट ,
तब आती है वापस मन में चैन की आहट ।

जब जाए वो स्कूल तो होती है फिकर ,
हर काम में होती है उसी का ज़िकर ।
माँ बेटी का रिश्ता होता है अनोखा ,
खट्टी,मीठी ,उलझती ,सुलझती ,चटपटा लेखा झोका ।

बेटी कि माँ होना होता नहीं है आसान ,
हज़ारों चिंताओं से रहती है एक माँ परेशान ।
ज़िन्दगी की धूप में न झुलसे ये कोमल मन उसका ,
बन जाए वो इतनी सख्त कि खुद अपना रास्ता बनाये पक्का ।
हर माँ की यही होती है अपनी बच्ची के लिए चाहत ,

बने उसकी बेटी शक्ति का स्वरुप ,दूर रहे हर आफत ,
और बनी रहे जीवन की मुस्कान और शरारत ।

16. त्योहार के दिन

त्योहार के दिन होते बड़े सुहाने ,
खुशियों को मिल जाते कई नए ठिकाने ।

जीवन के दौड़ धूप की छाँव है ये त्योहार ,
इंसान को देकर मीठी यादें , ये जोड़ते हैं परिवार।
कभी आरती कभी शंख कभी फूलों की बौछार ,
कभी दिए, कभी फुलझड़ी कभी रंगो के बहार,
कभी मिलनी तो कभी राबड़ी और मिठाइयों का मेला ,
हवा मे घुलती ख़ुशी की लहर ,हर पल लगता एक नई बेला।
हंसी के ठहाके तो कभी नाच गानो से खिलखिलाता आँगन ,
त्योहारों मे ख़ुशी से झूम उठता हर मन।

भाग्यशाली है हम, बारह महीनो मे मनाते हैं हम तेरह पर्व ,
हर मौसम की नई उमंग , होते हमारे देश मे इतने उत्सव ।

17. That Stage of Life

At a fateful moment, you realize,
You have reached that stage of Life,
Where ambitions don't matter anymore!
You feel like a stone within your core!

Being alone, feels divine,
Silence feels like gold and you shine!
There is a new journey of knowing you,
Speaking to clouds, trees, feel what they could have gone through.

These thoughts may seem insane,
Boundless questions fire up, difficult to tame!
You start questioning "Who am I?"
Just the way you did when you were a child!

There is a search within you that you follow,
Beyond the laughter, smiles and the sorrow!

What are we, from where have we come??

How did we thrive to the life we have become.

Many questions you ask your soul,
The mystery of life is tough to unfold.
This is the point you also understand,
What we have as life is a precious "garland"!

Made with the flowers of experiences and feelings,
With every end there comes a new beginning !

18. Its Okay!!!Women!!

Its okay to feel a certain way,
When you don't want to go away.
Its okay to stop and listen to your heart,
Understanding yourself is also an art.
Its okay to feel vulnerable,
You could be angry or irritable!
Its okay to let things and people go,
For peace within is also important to know!

Its okay that you cannot be the best every time
As you are human,you need to pause for the sunshine!

Its okay to feel weak and tired,
You also need love and feel cared.
Its okay if you cant be perfect,
Your well being ,you should not neglect!
Life teaches to embrace things as it comes,
And how you nurture yourself will decide what life
becomes..

So dear women, please love yourself , its Okay!
Happiness flourishes within , so smile and sail through
this foray!!

www.ingramcontent.com/pod-product-compliance
Lightning Source LLC
LaVergne TN
LVHW022031200926
848481LV00007B/2645
* 9 7 9 8 9 0 0 8 1 9 1 2 9 *